KISSING OTHER PEOPLE

OR

THE HOUSE OF FAME

KISSING OTHER PEOPLE

OR

THE HOUSE OF FAME

KAY
GABRIEL

NIGHTBOAT BOOKS
NEW YORK

ISBN: 978-1-643-62179-1

First American Edition—2023

Originally published in Australia in 2021 by Rosa Press.

Design and typesetting by Rosa Press
Text set in Swampy Hound and Baby Red

Cataloging-in-publication data is available from the
Library of Congress

Nightboat Books
New York
www.nightboat.org

Contents

Year Zeroes

If no ideas but in prisons we shall have no ideas
nor the city its bridges   for scare-quote arterial
say digestive or intestinal
       the blood is elsewhere and the circuit can't take
a pecunious shit   Brooklyn's coming to eat the 88th
our bedrooms, private hospitals, discharged
us onto the streets   well we ditched them first
       they had nothing left to teach us
     no Bon App no bedhead coffee
the nothing true except made actual gospel
      going into the meat world   Dear Cam:
      the commune turns 149 this May   Haiti as old as
invention   you and me as the 90s gruel
ours the waste and water piping ours say the car horns
outside black-mold NYCHA apartments
      ours from pretty Sunday Sunset Park
to MDC off Third
a feedback screech discrepant until no
cages is a singular truth
     "ours," so, everyone on and of them
       intent to disperse
swell and amplify   "metastasize"   delimit
the ideational non-place
where when you're back we'll be having rice and pulses
     hold in gasses   kiss and flip off the one or two
remaining pigs since two months back we put up an anti-
monument to the flaking shit-crust
     memory of cops and DOCs
and everyone passing it moons the empty space or flips
the bird or repossesses a torched
precinct in the absolute mode of quit your jobs

"STOFFWECHSEL"

rudely I am, Andy, addled with cold and this is an occasion
say for naps and dreaming as it turns out I dreamt about you,
the occasion of my poem, which is the reason for telling you
the epiphany of a poem called STOFFWECHSEL
this poem was by you in fact it was penned in your hand
it showed the evidences of your formal niceties say
deliberate refusal to break the line on
a fifty-cent word like "niceties"
indeed the cheeriest philologues could have
established to a skeptical audience it was indeed
your poem written by you
which you read to me by my feverish bed
in which I dreamt (U.S. English "dreamed")
of things like STOFFWECHSEL
the Frankfurt am Main wannabes' theoretical
centerpiece I'd prefer at a wedding or sickbed
Andy get ready for the good part
though I pause in relating the poem
to take Advil and water to continue relating the poem
called "STOFFWECHSEL" in which you intoned
GET UP POET IT'S TIME TO INGEST YOUR THEORY
the capital letters hammering even on the Starbucks
windows of my stuffy nose GET UP POET you said again
IT'S TIME TO INGEST YOUR THEORY
at which point conveniently there appeared in the poem
Advil and a glass of water to hand
the debt to Eliot is clear, even those
cheeriest of philologues agree:
Andy, your poem is superior
Eliot chose not to supply the reader with any
non-steroidal anti-inflammatory drugs at all
or acetaminophen, yours is an apothecary

more receptive to business which is how it comes that
this poem "STOFFWECHSEL"
is among other things manifestly yours not Tommy's
David's or even Kay's
not written by the four-piece suit
I metabolize nothing it comes right back
out with a child's persistence
Andy I tumbled out of the dream into the insistence
of a whole bottle of Advil I will never again
          have a headache this Feb.
a month in any case when I shall bear up in hopes of
the epiphany of your poem redux
the instructions on the bottle stipulating it
          is to be taken with food
toast e.g. or flavored ice or oyster crackers, say
in the Stoffwechsel of the age I'm feeling
          good enough to hurry up

Today I would like $25 to be a poet, but I won't get it. In dreams I own or rent or hole up in large barricaded properties, e.g. tonight a Hell's Angel under ambush in Bordentown, NJ. I circle a tree with daggers — what's the Tarot card for that? When the ritual's complete the tree will smithereen the heads of my haters, they've got me dead to rights but from up here they look like schoolteachers.

Or again I am a precocious witch in a private garden backyarded onto a spacious, elegant house. A sick unsightly mortgagess, I've kept the neighborhood kids from my property, batted their parents out of the house and cursed or murdered the ones who crossed me, and took the groceries they brought. Ripping someone else's bagels dunked in cream cheese, lick, chew, spit. I suppose I have a reason for how I'm carrying on, though I never manage to swallow the bites I stole and laundered, maybe from roommates. Now I'm a rentier — is this paranoia, fear or fantasy? Property appears under my feet, collectors meticulous at the door. One dollar sign, says Cam. Two dollar signs! Yes, I say, pronouncing the glyphs like a cash register. I wake up to an unpaid ambulance bill for my shredded knee.

We move out to start fresh, somewhere on a gorgeous budget. Bored with Latin, my students revolt for lunch. In Princeton, NJ, $5 gets you an initially fulfilling sandwich at Mamoun's Falafel, plus the guarantee you won't run into your boss. The sandwich falls apart in transit, the hot sauce gives you the shits. I regret nothing, dripping inside and out. As toppings they offer: pickles, olives, radishes. All three? they ask. Oh yes, I say. All three.

Thanks, you're right. I look forward to revising. I'll revise with your comments in mind. In another dream a tank top figure in pistachio shorts presides over a sink of undone dishes, and decides they've seen worse. I wake up in the late afternoon first rested then seizing with underemployed nerves, at quarter to four, can't remember why so fretful but would dearly like to puke on someone — maybe a reader, who has sent comments on a chapter while I slept.

I begin revisions with a grievance. Did I mean grief? My breasts spill out in a waiting room where I am at pains to produce edits on a draft. I reproduce my nausea at market — I call it inventive.

A Less Exciting Personism For The Less Fabulously Employed
with Cam Scott

About bathos they were spot-on, those studious pervs:
      In the path of totality the sun is
      blotched by a thumbprint
Things trade places on approach —
        look how easily it transforms into its opposite, a doctor
Is that my body odor or my roommate's kush?
      I can expect a response to my claim in 60 days, a *bzz*
Misspelled 'Moloch' as 'Mooch'
       and a *chk* on the other end of the line
       then a hold oh fuck
The staff room is for spoilers if not company,
      this field of sharers and squinters is versus containment:
a melancholy contractor loosens the bolts
on option of a second date
        however tidy, it gets between two gritting teeth!
Unpaid for months without so much as a promise
      But how can you really care
      if it vegetably improves them
I don't know the case law is this 'ghosting'?
      who have paid for an experience more in tuition
All that is solid waxes in the maw
      than the wage (mine) whose status is as dramatically
Months shy of centenary, they sell nostalgia, don't they
      in doubt as that experience is secured
They don't do no good and that's not nothing
      Do you know where your children
      are in structured leisure?
Democratic Centralism in the bedroom but a
roving census in the streets
      failed a test and I'm gay on the pedantic
      I mean pedagogic mound

The protest pens are full, we are state pets from ten to six
　　　　at least it happened over the phone, xo, the subdiscipline
blushed in the crush of our convictions
　　　　Graduate school (wheedling) a universal
　　　　basic, should you go
Decentering oneself, it was a decent reign
driving my racecar in reverse
　　　　as if a baggy anomie rolled its
　　　　translation in butter and crumbs
When the filthy rich lowball you are they flirting
　　　　"Romantically," avers a manager, then chokes
Lifting one leg at a time over the edge of the bed,
　　　　the opposite of improvement or that's the
　　　　intention I will have wanted to secure
A leaden burden with an eyelid for a book
　　　　I grade this I grade that
An analyst might say that one is habitually
late in order to assert control
　　　　veering to the edge of an even better estrangement
But I blame the MTA I assert nothing
　　　　contusion on a lawn in concert
　　　　everybody sleeps in a bed tonight

Blind Item

1. Peroration

Stephen Ira is in the bath!
Stephen Ira is ten feet tall!
Stephen Ira wears bright blue trunks!

The scandal Stephen Ira
The dandy Stephen Ira
The infamy, Stephen Ira

Stephen reads the poems of Roberto Bolaño,
       reverent in church.
Stephen reviews the Letters to James Alexander,
       and takes them to the zoo.
Stephen enjoys the personas of Dennis Cooper,
       bluely inside.

My invoice for 78 cents, Stephen Ira
My receipt for a whiskey rocks, Stephen Ira?
My rich deserts, do they look okay?

Stephen, musk-redolent
Stephen, multi-orgasmic
Stephen, quasi-violinist

Liker of Forster, Stephen Ira!
Delighter in Stein, Stephen Ira!
Pleased by Genet, Stephen Ira!

As Doctor of Dental Science (D.D.S.):
       thunderous, abrupt

As Philosophiae Doctor (Ph.D.):
    impressive in shorts
As laboratory scientist (???):
    moistly attentive

Plushly on the carpet, Querelle:
A loser of *jeux*, a cheat
Criminal in criminal body hair.

Transfixed at the mirror
and enjoying something made by her wife.
Alice, Gertrude, Gertrude, Alice, appetite.

More suggestive of infinity than any railway,
Stephen Ira! The Schlegels are upon us.
And what do you intend to do?

2. A Country Weekend

Stephen is late to catch our train. "Sorry," he says, "I was on my antique telephone in a nightgown. Guess the film!" But I let it slide. Why fight about it? We are going to the country. Breathy chit-chat gives us an auspicious start, but just as we sit down a spirit of the age appears neatly across the aisle with an inscrutable tome, which she folds across her knee. Accosted:

THE RAT RACE: Pipe down about your email! This is the quiet car! Lights the fuck out!

She makes a good point, so we pick up our sandwich wrappers. The next car features a granite bar, mood lighting, and crustpunk on the speakers. Ice-cubes in the shape of pearls rattle with our relentless forward motion. Isn't it glish, Stephen Ira — I open my mouth to say so.

GAVIN DEGRAW, TENDING BAR: I know you! You're that hot pants kids. Don't you have opinions? But I won't be having your business, Mary!

What to do when both of you are Mary? We have to agree, even our currency shares our proclivities, well-assed by moonlight. Shall we proceed to the lounge car, Stephen Ira?

Oh, for want of a fainting couch! Yet as we pass into the car I swoon onto a convenient chaise longue. When I come to Stephen is talking to a man in achingly tight pants. "Me too," I say. Stephen makes introductions: "Kay! Come meet The Real Deal. He plays piano for the lounge society." The lounge society? Sure: women all around us chomp on fat cigars.

Sofas stuffed against loveseats recall so many bumper cars, an afternoon on the Seine. The Real Deal strikes up Porter —

THE REAL DEAL: You're sublime — you're the Analytic — you're a lime — for a churlish critic —

This Real Deal tickles my nose, Stephen Ira, can we keep him? But then the rest of the lyrics momentarily escape me out of embarrassment. Farewell, tight pants! Away we fly to the following car. The train, indeed, devours the countryside hurtling on towards — but here we have arrived in our own private bureaucrat.

CREAM OF THE CROP, Private Bureaucrat: What's the big idea? Which among you frequents the state capital? Show me some plastic! This form belongs to another decade! What is the glyph beneath your port of entry stamp? Who sews the pants? Who lays the tracks? Who sets this thing in motion?

Thus baffled by questions we debark quite by accident at the last stop on the weekend, and were forced to start all over when, just now, the telephone began to ring —

3. Matins

I brush my teeth with the writer Stephen Ira

I masturbate with the writer Stephen Ira

I run laps with the writer Stephen Ira

I tend bar with the writer Stephen Ira

I pull the plug on the writer Stephen Ira

I dilate next to the writer Stephen Ira

Am in cahoots with the writer Stephen Ira

brew coffee for the writer Stephen Ira

stamp stamps with the writer Stephen Ira

I lick letters to the writer Stephen Ira

I sext the writer Stephen Ira, on accident

Am up all night with the writer Stephen Ira

Am at pains to determine, Stephen Ira,

My morning schedule with the writer Stephen Ira

with the writer Robert Duncan

with the writer Kylie Minogue

with the writer David Wojnarowicz

with the writer Stuart Hall

with the writer Helen Adam

with the writer Dionne Warwick

with the writer Heiner Müller

with the writer Sky Ferreira

with the writer Arthur Russell

with the writer Larry Levan

with the writer Jacqueline Susann

with the writer Louis Zukofsky

with the writer Samuel "Chip" Delany

with the writer G. "W.F." Hegel

with the writer Gaius Valerius Catullus

with the writer Carly Rae Jepsen

with the writer Friedrich Schlegel

with the copycat August Wilhelm Schlegel

with the utopian Helen Schlegel

with the symbol Margaret Schlegel

with the pregnant Schlegel

with the perilously rural Schlegel

with the upbeat low-rent Schlegel

with the Schlegel Stephen Ira

and the Schlegel Leonard Bast

and the Schlegel Leonard Bookcase

4. Noises Set in Motion

Like machinery *aufhob* manufacture i.e.:
preserved and cancelled, "superseded"
since "sublated" is (a nitpick?) a table reserved for G.W.F.
and his friend G.W.F. Hegel, it's fancy,
it's latinate, it has a determinate origin,
it wears elaborate socks, it incorporates the thread
from its socks into its person, we might suggest:
"sublate" is a little gay.

Thus "reproduces," "blots out,"
"abstracts" — like machinery and manufacture thus today
who can tell the bather from the bath?
And would you like one?
And would you like to tell your friends?
And Stephen Ira, where is he?

Goodnight, Rimbaud

1.

I rush out into the street to be a stylish bag

        Venus in escrow plus a pink

    landscape spooned on toast

I also rush out to be a turd

    fan letters may be addressed to Kay Gabriel

    ℅ Turd Terrace

    Brooklyn, New York

    112-UP-YOURS

No autographs, please,

        I am only a famous bust!

"depicting Joan Jett or Rimbaud"

    gossip the museum plaques, then break for lunch.

The controversy renders friendships null and void,

has resulted in a divorce

may yet bankrupt modern art

I do it for my fans, I'll kiss my chips now

I'll touch all my stuff before they bring me to heel

Riding shotgun on the millennium seaboard

I busted the Atlantic, oops

2.

Double-parked in Sarnia, Barrie, Kitchener-Waterloo

townships of destiny

and not a parkade between them

a "multistory parking garage"

Canadian English hiccups international

stars of stage and finance

Margaret, Justin, Elizabeth

toothful bank towers   oh! big boys!

hot pink armpits of Canada, you're number one

Dear vexatious reader:

I am not a Margaret or a rounded vowel

I'm a handsome idiot of Paradise bearing good news:

I love pink

                          I parked my car in that colour

3.

Lady, I'm not Rimbaud, that's my roommate

    Mon ami, Rimbaud

        he creams the sofa bed in pink jorts

Cranks the AC to 68 and puts on the National

Rimbaud smells of warm pineapple

    Heads out to shows with the gas on

    "Hey, man   what the fuck"

    clucks the stove, soiled in bright blue hair.

His rent check bounces —
          "Dad moved some cash around

    I'll make up for it   fries on me"

Rimbaud sprawls in a diner booth making face

    masks out of napkins and vinegar

I order the promised fries and a very magenta slaw

Malibu Arthur gets onion rings, extra pickles, a french

      dip sandwich diagonally sliced and the crusts cut off

warbles behind his condiment sheets like a soggy ghost

When he sticks to the couch we take him to the cleaners

      Rimbaud comes back like a two-for-one deal

          squeak! SQUEAK!

"Oh, *Arthur*"

          he combs detergent out of his hair

4.

Laundry day! start strong and hit the suds

      the city pinches its bladder shut till early Sat-

      urday A.M. then lets er rip *con brio*

Oh   it's metaphysical!

my boobs boing across Flatbush like two well-
      coiled mattresses

I forget which one is Kelsey Grammar

      from up here the boroughs look like a pothos plant

      it rains on the skylight a *sarabande pathétique* in D

Miss Long Nineteenth Century walks her poets on the beach

      stuffs them in with her brights and shut the door

           between loads my roommate has lots to say

"Goodnight, Rimbaud"

"Goodnight, Aesthetic Education"

5.

O Captain, my Commuter Rail

Under pressure in the OR they rewire my head

now I'm:

- left handed
- beautiful
- and *never* have to go back to Canada

A woman with hair like Hugh Grant's sister in *Notting Hill* instructs me all night in the simplicity of love then admits she's bored of heartbreak and leaves me to wake up

Before that walking down a large beautiful street say a boulevard sunny where all the trees have saved us from fossil capitalists the pavement is broken in the middle and we rush forward into that kind of street on that kind of day I feel like crying but no I don't I get up I find two people named Fuck the Police arm wrestling at a table Stephen says you have to get in on this, don't you know what time it is

I guess I don't instead I dream of the Latin verb *errare* meaning to be mistaken the translation in the dream is "you're pretty" and a fashion designer names a dress "This is the Poem of the Mammalian Surface"

Soon I meet one character called the art-ascendiant and another who has the face of Macauley Culkin in *Party Monster*, I have elaborate plans to get back at them both meanwhile as our school activity we are all climbing a tall structure to a theater where cops in riot gear yell at us if we try to get out of our seats, I find out scandalous gossip from the suspicious but hot art-ascendiant including that Macauley Culkin is a spousal hire and decades older than he's supposed to be

I am having an affair with an older married woman whose house is full of paper and screens, her husband is perfectly nice but a bore, but soon D. and Z. arrive and in order to avoid them I leave in the wintry ice without my shoes and fairly run to catch the bus and on waking I note this is a "dream I somehow resent" though not as much as I do the doctors who refused to treat patients and when they were forced to answer why they said it was because they were the children of Psychic TV

Marie and I are going to teach a course by night and I have not thought up provisions for people to read the materials in total darkness, Marie thinks this is a grave error and that the LSD-tripping movers who are gonna schlep my stuff by bicycle 40 miles will therefore miss out when they are forced to camp out under the stars with all my earthly possessions and no firewood

I dream of isolated reading groups conducted over video where we're very grateful then very frustrated to sift through material like hunks of matzo balls we carve up with our spoons, they look like large tan asses or the backs of calves and eventually we admit our frustrated feeling at the intransigence of the task where once we were confident of the pleasure of hearing voices over the phone

At a summer camp somehow for adults only I am being moved from one house to another for undisclosed administrative reasons and before anyone moved they had to change the gross bags of soap in the soap dispensers, Celia had promised to help but is nowhere present until finally I hear her arrive in the hall along with the attendants who will shepherd me to my next inevitable apartment

Then I dream the same dream again only it's not summer camp but a childhood home and this time the reason for the move-out is that I am a jilted lover, my sister takes my apartment and fills it with my sometime boyfriend N. the observant Jewish henna artist, he hugs me he's gotten very tall and almost masculine I'm still attracted to him he says I hate this as in I suppose how awkward it would be to date my sister after dating me and I feel relatively more chilled out about the whole thing but still squeezed out like paste from a tube both of us worried somehow about our wombs

Before that I dream of mass unrest at the very near Canadian border, a crowd embarks to engage in it too but once there I stay in the apartment of friends, a gothic haunted building, I have a flip phone I can't use despite Hal's patient instructions, Mike sends me anxious messages I continually forget to read. One of my hosts plays the violin, another has a pet lizard they keep on a leash and the hotel staff make you get a dangerous animal license even to hold it. Mike is going to come find me in the morning, is it morning yet, have I missed him, but I proceed alone however briefly until I am in a snow-covered landscape in a coward's house refusing to answer the door and even after we admit the cowardice of the entrance we use several elaborate locks to keep it that way

I am sitting down on a park bench by night underneath a bridge like the George Washington or Verrazano to eat a box of butter chicken like a puzzle or a game of chess with Rosario who I think is irritated to be instrumentalized but she plays the game of chess-chicken very well until it is possible to identify whether and where we will both become sick and then we walk back together an abandoned and garbage-strewn river in the sense of its not having been like this even recently and that this was the result of foolish and avoidable action by the state

then I am on the phone with a friend who cites a
poetic authority to say that talking on the phone is
both useless and dangerous and I try to talk them
down I am singing Fireman by Jawbreaker but fail to
persuade, all night I dream of small glowing circles,
you have to connect them to talk at all

I have friends on Fire Island who are lending me the key to their house to use if ever I like. I don't know them well, they may even be more friends of friends, and as I approach through the warm pool water I am careful to ask kindly for their key — they seem sweet enough — which I also intend to copy surreptitiously in a mold of silicone putty, then I take the ferry to their home, let myself in and touch all of their things

A troop of actors mount a play, Ibsen or something, no staging we sit in a row in a church. It's cold I put on the play with two different casts but doubts have been raised about my love life or maybe the love life of the tortured bony man who plays the lead, on waking I recognize the BBC-famous Reeve Carney, but then one woman before the second performance confesses to being the mother of the child born out of wedlock and the church despite her prayers for mercy falls apart around her and the director who was also the priest comes downstairs to reveal it was all his trap

I dream of a snow-covered field full of schoolchildren and friends all of us off from work and schooling there are prizes if you make it around the track balancing on your skis as if on a snowboard and as I try this out I have to shout to my students and friends, Stephen is among them, to go left, left, a little more left so I don't fall, I almost make it but wipe out at the last second and Patrice has brought specialty candles we can use to light small patterns of Greek fire on the lake

then Patrice and Matty are wiping down everyone's hands with turmeric before they enter the house as a social worker I am colleagues with my sister at a shelter attempting to rehabilitate and adopt neighborhood kittens, she waylays me in the elevator and thrusts a cat on me she says is now my responsibility and I do take it and become its confidante meanwhile I think she's acting willfully in an attempt to sabotage me and steal my boyfriend who she's never met and when I confront her about this betrayal she speaks more intently into her phone, eventually I tackle her as if we were kids I say *this is an HR complaint* she seems ready to acknowledge her poor behavior but I wake up before she can confess

I dream of a beautiful but fragile friendship that cannot withstand the pain of one party (one of the friends is me) or the possibility of exposure to flu. I know my friend would like to withdraw from me, in the dream I act as if this is because of my overbearing Patti Lupone histrionics but secretly I suspect I'll deserve it and still I pretend that everything is normal and sing a Broadway song underground as I approach every room they are living in, in the dark and confusion, the song goes *you're LATE shithead you've got another DATE shithead*, it's a song about a cruel wronged woman and I sing it at my former friend's door as they try to indicate I'm wasting my time and theirs even though an important part of the Broadway act is I must be throwing knives at all times

even when I am exposed to the virus, bags and bags of it lined up underground as if for transport on a garbage truck, a suspicious character dials me and asks how could I fail to recognize them when they saw me at Happyfun only 70 minutes before, I try to hang up on them but the call keeps going, I would smash my phone but now it's time to teach which today takes the form of helping my students kill the bugs in their housing unit since somehow Malina and I have been granted permission to teach once again but I have forgotten all my books and pens and must exit through a yard to retrieve them over and over, then our students have done no reading as if we had dreamt up the several weeks of the already-past term, we exit into the daylight where I dream-drive capably until a man climbs in the back as if ordering a cab telling me to drive in a certain direction but I only crash us on purpose so badly do I mistrust him

Before that I dream I am with Stephen and Liam at their kitchen table sorting my prescriptions, they say you have to hunt for the embarrassing pills

NYC Dyke March takes place in the form of a small crew departing from Brooklyn, we proceed laboriously up stone-cut staircases onto the Williamsburg bridge to finish the march in Manhattan, I ask everyone if they've ever been to a dyke march so small before, the staircases are so hard to climb sometimes you're just holding onto railings with your hands and then in order to advance onto the footbridge you have to knock on an iron grate and a small creature lets you proceed after you leap over a deep chasm down to the highway but I'm sitting on top of it and wondering how good or bad it might be to drop all the way down

until I arrive at a large party Inferno or Spectrum brushing past a nameless jerk I recognize, hating him fully, sure he had seen me, intent on appearing hotter and different

In the company of several friends and characters from Mario Kart we play a real-life version of the game together and also manoeuver our way out of Hell; first we have to dash through haunted levels, then we push ourselves up a spacious and well-lit elevator shaft, this is what Yoshi excels at, Yoshi so excited at the power of friendship he sends us collectively high as the roof high as a building, it's like a special on kids' TV explaining something about collaboration, the rules of the escape from Hell specified that contestants couldn't prepare the materials necessary to beat a level in advance of actually doing so and we therefore had to be practiced but seem unpracticed and act very affable as we pull out of the driveway of my childhood home

T. delivers a submission to the newsletter, it's a mound of hummus on a plate, actually several mounds and the newsletter staff is gathered in my Ridgewood living room and he seems apologetic but everyone loves tawny affable hummus

a vaccine is recently developed except after
you get the shot you have to take the pink pills
several times also I am living in Toronto and
I don't want to take the pills instead I ration
them, go into the world and knock on doors

until Morgan explains the histories of Genesis
P-Orridge and Lady Jaye and says in reference
to the four pink crumpled drink tickets or
raffle tickets I have and am refusing to use that
I'd better hand them over so she can use them
if I won't though their purpose is so obscure

Before that I talk with a staff of teachers about "lonelies" meaning thoughts and "onlies" meaning feelings, we agree these are sentimental and romantic and there are very few of them but still they're critical to attend to

Gia and I are leading a chamber music practice session late at night in a building with many classrooms and a pool, I am carrying the violin outside of its case, the bow hairs have started to deteriorate very badly, I excuse myself to fix the damage wandering into an all-gender space with toilets but it's flooded and full of pool water, my E string snaps and I look for the packet I bought at a convenience store to replace it but I must have forgotten it's only a packet of sugar, I find Gia and exit again into the night soaked from the flood I hold up the busted violin and when I say I'm going home I can't take it she seems actually very understanding

I dream of a show of paintings, Stephen and Liam are present, the paintings are all of my friends or other transsexuals, I want to purchase a picture of Bryn but I don't know if that's appropriate and then the man running it won't take my money anyway though I think in the dream I wanted to give it to Mike

an overseas correspondent wants my insights on a newly discovered
Kathy Acker novel and though this man is a guaranteed fuckhead I can't
disappoint I must run to the airport up a large miles-long wooden platform
with many different obstacles and rail lines on a bright sunny day and then
I run past Jake Gyllenhaal and he asks me what movies I've been in lately,
the airport is just out of reach I'll really have to bolt the final distance and
I feel very confident of doing so

> all the way into a full-body scanner like for drugs in
> an airport except it's for illness and you place it by
> your door and to my own waking embarrassment
> in the confines of the dream I am a fan of a federal
> regulation that means you have to use it always,
> Mike is less sure. It blows cold mountain air at you,
> I say, it's curative

A little later I am underground in a video game dungeon and I
don't know if I'm supposed to be fighting or fucking the final
boss or if he's supposed to be fighting or fucking me

Beforehand I dream that the scientist mom from *A Wrinkle in Time* is a lesbian and that one of the transdimensional middle-aged witches moves into her house and becomes her lover for thirty years, after she dies or disappears I must go through her boxes to sort and discard her possessions and books during which time I learn the whole story of the affair from the mild heroic daughter

I am planning to gift Cam a bright pink book
for his birthday and then he pulls his own
copy out of his bag returning from Canada

where I'm now a renter in a house like my
parents' with a lawn, Stephen lives on the top
floor where he pokes his neighborly head out the
window and a friend handsome and masculine
who delights in sweets lives in the basement, I
go down and let myself into his rooms and
cultivate his friendship but mainly so I can leave
with bags of dessert whose recipe lists I check
nonetheless for whatever I can't have like whey
and eggs, Stephen comes out and says there you
are and tells me to pick up my phone and I find
that instead of searching for me he'd asked many
friends for my whereabouts when the whole
time I was only a couple floors down from him
scrounging up chocolate

Then Conrad exits and is full of information
about war, deals, credit, amenities, ore, gold,
trading, debt and derivatives, you may not
understand these things he says but you will
touch them for the rest of your life

Mike and I are invited to a friend's house where we will be photographed in our underwear but first we share a meal in an unfamiliar apartment where I am sure I live now and then we bike in the rain many miles to our photoshoot and our hair isn't ruined at all, then there are many other people in the photographer's apartment and she turns out all the lights and shuts the blinds and makes meticulous notes of her light meter reading, its numbers are impossible in that level of darkness but I suppose she knows what she's doing, I have the vague sense that the shoot is a front for us all eventually fucking but I don't ask and wait my turn and when I wake up I am ashamed to remember my first fear was whether I'd look small enough for myself

Stephen and Liam are leaving the many
floors of their apartment to a production of
Macbeth that will take place in the Myrtle-
Broadway JMZ, recently converted into
an operatic station, meanwhile there's a
younger woman with us I feel surprisingly
attracted to and then as we begin to fuck I
discover she's thin as a communion wafer
and surprisingly trans, I'm embarrassed
to accidentally live out the narrative of a
shocked and clueless chaser as if I'd never
scoffed at this character's severe idiocy,
Stephen says slow down tiger or put it away
but I don't reply, instead I go upstairs to
fuck my bony crush but worry throughout
the dream that I have lost the entirety of my
vaginal depth from never dilating

Only now I'm rushing to catch the bus away from the door where our
ideological enemies are sure to catch us, if I do not get on this bus I will
have to walk all night in the dark, I make it up six flights of stairs and text
Jo frantically asking if they can stall the bus for me since I'm both a doctor
and a cat

By night I lie in the grass outside and although it's still February I am periodically covered in mating bugs but it's only a little bit gross, mostly I throw off the earthworms and say you go there and there

Then the Vicomte and Marquise from *Dangerous Liaisons* campily enclose themselves in a chamber they cannot unlock from the inside, there's a door but when you lift it you only see drywall, the Marquise intends for them to stay in this room past the point of their fear but who will break them out when they want to leave

Not me I'm too busy discovering for the very first time
the connection between *two* and *doubt*, this insight a
necessary step before I proceed down a Hegelian way of
despair, in the dream it begins on Halsey St.

In the dream I play someone like Viggo Mortensen in a baroque haunted house that is also an opera hall. It's very large, as in, it could host a writing retreat. I am attempting to leave, I do not like my fellow actors, and I say insulting things about the house. *Everyone says this staircase is remarkable* I say, standing and feeling as if I might fall to the distant ground, *But what's so remarkable about it, you say that about anything,* disembodied hands emerge from the staircase and begin to jostle me, to grab my collar and wring my neck, I slide all the way down to the foyer with a large man who reads a magazine advising him not to allow his sons to listen to Joni Mitchell

Before that I find myself cutting roses in a bourgeois garden privy to the comings and goings of its residents, a couple manages the garden in their medium-sized but keeping up appearances house, the wife is plump and beloved and neglected, the husband conniving and sinister, the wife disappears and the husband, effete and philandering, is considered a suspect and a flight risk, he elegantly dissuades the investigators of his role in the crime though he certainly did it but then he breaks his neck too, the roses are a delicate pink

A surgeon is operating on my nipples to make my aureolas smaller and after botching the job says, "Well, they're symmerical" and I don't know if she means *symmetrical* or *spherical* or both

I am exploring a large and ugly school building with a fistful of pills I must take right away but the only vessel for water I'm holding is the teapot I shoplifted and in the bathroom the sinks are full of brackish hot water, all of the pills are already in my mouth although I don't understand how they could possibly have not begun to taste appalling, they're mild and a little sweet and when I wake up I realize I'm tasting my spit

Stephen and Hal and I are heading to various all-night parties, Stephen is carrying around a large paint container of edible glitter-filled paint in which one very strong beautiful colour like a red or gold is paired with many other colours in the pieces of glitter visible in the solution, some of them quite a charming admixture some garish or even ugly and you never knew what colour of glitter you were going to get when you sprayed the edible paint trough an airbrush machine, still we take our chances and paint everything including a music stand and the insides of our drinks and even the lighter fluid in our lighters, when Stephen sprays it the paint comes out beautiful with beautiful glitter and when I do the beautiful glitter has finished passing through the nozzle and I must content myself with an inferior colour, Stephen doesn't seem to mind, I think by this point Hal has long since gone to sleep tired out from the willful spraying and we are hanging out in a small dark room and it is bright and sunny on the driveway outside even though we are certainly in the middle of the night and the much advertised party has turned out to be nothing at all, Niel is apparently on his way even as Dagan has been ominously summoned to have to speak to his manager

My family present in an apartment to celebrate some major holiday like Pesach everyone is very drunk and all my gay friends are around me too to congratulate me on being the star of the dance floor but mostly I was very confused and wanted to go home, my sister and I have a sense of social obligation and we sit down to eat a mountain of food but I remember that although it was very expensive it was also very bad, a challah like a cold white mountain of meal, then I must negotiate a large entertainment deck complete with DVD and VHS players while my dad wants to lift me onto his shoulders and I must hug many people from up there without knocking over the TV

Finally we hear a large crash and look out the window across the river (we are Bolsheviks in Petrograd and must wait for the right moment to make revolution) and on this summer night we see joyous aimless crowds ripping apart an ice cream truck and pushing its contents into the river, there is also a man here I badly want to kiss but I am too busy being congratulated for something I haven't done

I dream of an upside-down teapot that is supposed to be specifically Jewish but I don't understand how the hot water doesn't all rush out through its open foot

Then I am on the run with a man who claims to be my father but in his beard he is too handsome, he is also a doctor and we could be in grave danger for all the surgeries he has given my freshly beautiful face, we arrive in the southwest where we shall be free of police pursuit but here there's nothing to do but answer the door

I also have a sister who died after being born with a congenital respiratory problem such that if you pressed anywhere on a line around her neck she wouldn't be able to breathe at all and someone did not know this and pressed and panicked and she tragically suffocated and now we must return her car to the rental dealership without being suspected

Then I dream of a jam made from cherries and zucchini, I am spooning it out of the jar and intend to eat it but think it will probably taste so bad, why would you make it in the first place, then I tell Mike about the dream and he says the colour of the jam would probably be an unsettling brown and I say yes but really it was all neon red like a maraschino cherry jar except for the lumps of zucchini

Only now Liam has arrived late to Shiv and Diana's party to tell me that Patricia Highsmith's racecar is the source of all my poems but I can't drive it

Oh I am a boy in the 80s in high school on an island I am fucking my bully routinely actually he's fucking me describing my tight ass for the camera and we are unwisely using vaseline for lube so it's very teenaged after all and then he has a drink in his hand and we have saved the narrative world, its people and oceans, through the intervention of our impressive fucking, I worry it's selfish as we go to fuck on a roof and also I haven't douched so won't there be shit everywhere just like with the vaseline but my bully doesn't seem to mind in this Valentine's card I send to myself

I dream of three celebrities roughly associated with the past, present and future but we aren't allowed to know their names, just they have agreed to be in our next theatrical production of the Oresteia, which Stephen is going to direct. The middle one looks suspiciously like Barbra Streisand and the final one's face we won't even see for the audition, we just know her tragic backstory and on that basis must decide whether and how to cast her and if she's lost or improved her sometime prodigious talent

Then I am taking a cab to the airport in Toronto which I am sharing with a man I do not know but somehow despise, my fellow cabrider must now drive from the backseat, he's a wanker I hate being stuck with him to spite him I pretend I'm getting married, then he begins to insult me too and calls me a wife and I reveal the marriage plot was just a joke to ironize him, he says you have no scruples if anyone backs you into a corner you pretend you're married to them or to someone famous and I fly at him through the air of an underground mall shouting *MRS HARRY STYLES MRS PENN BADGLEY*

I dream of a cheap substance that hardens especially fast and can be used to mass-produce lines of elevated rail, Danny and Grace wait patiently as I finish constructing a copy of the M train, Grace says this was a test of my integrity and memory but I passed and she will help me banish one bad thing about New Jersey as a result, Jackie is present and says I told you, we are all to be socially remembered

I am making outmeal outdoors in a metal bowl suspended above a small campfire in a suburban garden but I must both hide the evidence and rescue my friend from the villainous man in an ugly cap who's been snooping around here, he keeps coming around to kick over my stand and terrorize my oatmeal set-up but soon I'll get him and it'll be *pow!* right to the moon!

Driving my car, a tractor-trailer, through the corridors of a school building in San Diego, when I resurrect myself in this video game I will have to collect my body from this nothing-growing landscape and my truck which I abandoned in a school corridor will surely have been towed

In a bid to solve Brooklyn's void of DIY space several friends and I discover ourselves proprietors of the next one, in a former car wash, you crawl on hands and knees through swaying plastic sheets and run for sheer delight in a cavernous sometimes twisting series of rooms lit only by black light though I suspect the owner only leased us the space on the implication that my flirts would culminate in a genuine seduction and I'd fuck him after all

I am staying at a friend's apartment overnight before a major event like defending a doctorate, an apartment with many levels so maybe it's a manor house, the friend is very rich and gifts me a bottle of wine from his baroque wine cellar, the wine used to belong to Henry James, he tells me its value too. *Three hundred whole-ass dollars for a wine bottle* someone else says incredulously but I didn't pay it what do I know

Macy is looking for release from certain social obligations, we learn that the easiest way to do so is to encase yourself in a sugar coating but to take caution for the change might be permanent and you would be perpetually candied

I enter a house with a famous mystery writer on the edge of retirement, in the dream she's also my mother but I can't remember her name. It's not our house, so we might have to break in, and while she fumbles for the light I surmise she means to kill me, we enter the kitchen and I dream-fire dream-bullets towards her from my expert gun but they don't hit she just turns around and starts to dissolve like a large caramel

One footballer kicks another's head in over dating the same girl but the head dissolves into a dog bowl of bones and some teeth and for the ritual to work you had to stand inside it on one foot

I receive a transmission from Rylee in space who's setting off on a long journey falling through the disused tunnels of an abandoned space vessel, she flaps into a cold video game sun in a lemon of a spacecraft with holes in the wings

I'm swimming with a friend awkward in glasses in a small secret pool inside a classroom nobody knows about except us, there are white boards and markers and there's the pool and I am texting Cam about an unlikely probable and poorly formed idea, he gently disagrees, I leave my backpack floating on a ceramic step where it gets just a little damp but my phone is dead forever and my friend sucks in air through his judgmental teeth

A young Joseph Gordon-Levitt catches sight of me in a supermarket aisle spooning large embarrassing volumes of tomato soup into my mouth but I shoot him a look that's like *so what*

Before that I dream of one drag queen fingering another, aggressively attractive, who has her face still on but her wig off and tights pulled down beneath her thighs and who is lying on the floor fiercely jerking off as the former slams only one finger lacquered nail and all inside her, but the bottom looks almost as if her orgasm hurts her, shooting over her own abs and the pained expression on her climactic face

I encounter a supply of vacuum-sealed bread and raisins in large wooden food cabinets for a human life underground while outside it's the desert everywhere like on Dune or something and you get around in it by riding big tractors with large stone or concrete wheels huge like a building or a drum but when the packers of the food vacuum-sealed its secrets it was probably the desert rather than the mill they were mourning

Now I'm telling Will the sordid details of my non-affairs with leathermen and he taunts me in reply by singing the commercials for candy bars and chocolate bars

Everyone is a popular and devious news correspondent known by name and astrological sign and when you enter a room these details of curious biography are disclosed by the appearance of an illuminated manuscript page visually available to everyone no matter if you like it or don't, I think I don't

Before that I dream I live in a large house, maybe the Elle Woods sorority house from *Legally Blonde*, full of many people and flooded with celebratory blue light, either for New Year's or a graduation. Before midnight I walk around impressing many gay men who believe I am one of them, with my suddenly massive delts. One wants me to grow up into a handsome individual and encourages me to spend the night working out, a series of impossible exercises swinging off the arms of a gymnastic bench in the air. I do it for him, probably because of his strong jowls and beady big eyes and floppy hair, it's so easy impressing these dream people I think I'll walk around and do it all night

though problems arise when I realize I have keys to the downstairs apartment and also some of their mail, but there are new tenants living there we haven't met or seen all summer. I deposit a letter that I believe must talk about me, and since I want to know what it says I return a couple hours into the celebration to open it and read its contents, only just then a new roommate arrives and I sneak back into the party, letter and all, and after narrowly avoiding a confrontation with her plump protective sister I can't think how to return it: do I admit my petty theft and deception or attempt to put the letter back on its shelf and no one will notice? Undecided I walk around in unseasonable blue light without a solution I find myself carrying the letter into unaccountable situations, like I'll still be doing in the next dream

I participate in the production of a laboratory drug, you have to fry it twice in the shape of a blue hexagonal tortilla to get the high and on the first test at night by the streets I eat many and felt very guilty, a friend was bootlegging or back-engineering the drug chips out of blue tortilla flour that I liked so much. The second time I didn't get anywhere near so high but then I think I missed that precious feeling, the second time we were all more mature and prepared it without sandwiches and even then I felt high enough lying in fear that I couldn't go anywhere though I certainly had places to be

like walking the aisles of a grocery store spritzing the shelves with a spray bottle and covering them in chili powder especially the bottles of corn oil

Before that I dream that as a kid all of my birthdays are planned months or even years in advance down to the activities and kinds of cake and frosting but I am always sick on the birthday itself so I grow to dread it and to seek the company of other anti-birthday children, I make an anti-birthday trip and end up in a city I do not recognize like Chicago passed out on the street with a friend both of us too drunk to find our hotel mere blocks away and Katia must ply the taxi with riddles to carry us home

I have a whole alphabet or rolodex of possible dreams
and there's some repetition so you can even share them
with people and have them all at once, Mike and Ezra
and I in a row dreaming one called C for Charmed or G
for Demerol, in the dream it was called Gemerol

I roll down a hill to get to LAX, well, why did I try to get
here going the wrong way on the DC red line, travelling
with Connie who I think delights in my mistake though I
worry about my gently sleeping communally raised baby I
have left back at the karaoke house full of oogles

Lying down with A., no baby here, it's a sex dream.
Charming in leather accoutrements they ask if I want
to dream-suck their dream-dick and I say yes, it's long
like a thin almond or brazil nut and we're lying on an
elaborate bedspread printed with the underside of large
plants, they come in my mouth and I realize the bed
belongs to Blanche from *The Golden Girls*

Before that David Bowie and Bruce Springsteen were women Mike's dad had dated, who stuffed their crotches with socks and put on drag king wigs for the sake of the act, it was understood that like on Broadway nobody got to be David Bowie or Bruce Springsteen forever even if you originated the role and every New Year's Mike would wait for them to come into his bedroom (Mike was a child) and kiss him good morning

I live in a house with Mike and maybe our children and Ezra the cat and Ezra's evil double, it's my grandparents' house filled with ceramic tchotchkes on a dead street outside Barrie, ON. Mike and I are trying to have a baby he runs his fingers down my belly and says *getting there* but I shoot him a look so he changes his mind, and just in time for I've got a hideous temper, for instance suspecting Ezra's evil cat double of harbouring my grandparents' ill will I resolve to break its neck and when I do, laboriously, the head comes partly off leaving gore splatters on the clean but ugly rug, how will I explain this to my cousin who lives in the house in her peasant skirts and hateful attitude and who is not home but surely arriving very soon

I dream of spilling many liquids and of being very warm, uncomfortably warm in a house surrounded by water, accessible only by hopping on the tops of poles sunk deep underwater and in fact you have to hop on one foot. I am explaining something to Ry and to a dorky anonymous friend in a baggy foul-smelling sweater who is not at all approving of the story I am attempting to explain but Stephen must publish a second memoir about both the house and being Robin Williams's son

Cam shows up late after an evening out, is forced to speed-clean a kitchen over a rare recording of Bernadette Mayer playing Sibelius, it's a little comic watching him scoop brown sugar back into the cabinets or it would be if he weren't under extreme pressure, that's the name of his new band

I dream of orange cake of two different kinds, the kind you have when you're seeing each other (you lift it up and it sags down the middle like a sack) and the kind for authentic love, so small and satisfying it's barely there. I tell Mike we should keep on eating orange cake but not, indicating the sagging kind, not this one

I left a great mess of garbage in a church and went upstairs to see a play or a dress rehearsal for one, it was fine for me to be there without paying I thought because it's a dress rehearsal and so also fine for me to crawl around on the floor like a baby, all of the actors are close friends and classmates, when I leave I can hear them gossiping about me but it's not unkind, then I pick up all the garbage. By now I am on the balcony above the sanctuary but it's bright, very bright, and all wooden, I collect the trash including a broken glass positioning it so as not to cut anyone and discover a very convenient garbage chute going down many storeys, however far I can imagine, but even so the smell almost makes me faint, I drop the trash in and swoon backwards over the balcony

Aaron Cometbus is my dad and turns back into a roadie, a big beefy guy who cracks his knuckles and pushes away the fans whenever he can and says he's embracing success for his wife and child, I stand in somebody's TV room and my dad the roadie stands at a coffee table or counter looking for someone to threaten, of the members of the band none have kids except him, his family man status a closely guarded secret, he's a secret ascetic with his share of the t-shirt sales the better to support me and a woman with a large bosom and a halo of blonde hair I don't recognize as my mother

Engaged in a show of strength Ben hammers stuff into his head to impress his hot girlfriend but his insurance refuses to pay for the damages including a lip of flesh that has developed around one especially broad nail he hammers into his temple just over his ear, the other nails appear in montage, one in his shoulder blade and he flexes for us, the denial is read in voiceover — *Because the candidate knowingly inserts foreign objects into his body* — he doesn't seem very upset but of course he should get his fucking money

I am a songwriter but very bad at my job,
not a singer-songerwiter, chasing a singer
through the angular white corridors of a
music studio building somehow without
microphones, a colleague spots someone
famous, a famous singer, is it Tyler the
Creator? He goes into the bathroom and
the colleague waits for him outside, we are
so late, in a stairwell two women arrive at
a passable riff, I'm going to be fired I think

Walking down past a short wall or long
bench where very many famous people with
university jobs are sitting having lunch in
middle school and McKenzie summons me
down to the end, *Kay*, she says, *come meet
Donna*, Mike says forget them they're at
beauty cunt school and Harron says can I
bring enough for the wedding

Before that I dream that many brothers and sisters live in a suburban house up a grassy knoll or maybe we were X-Men or in a band. I joke to a brother that I've behaved so poorly that I deserve to have my bike stolen and then he really steals it but reveals it was just a prank, he hid the bike under the knoll and then I scream at him for fooling many strangers on the internet into believing what I had believed although I had elsewhere written approvingly about this brother as a "man of sane mind"

I dream of a paste you cut with a spoon spread all over the walls of a sumptuous edible home and you say I am going to take this to the Northrop medical doctor or you say I am taking mine to the tincture touchup artist

Rosario says to the landlord she can't pay the rent to move in but what if she puts a fresh $10 bill in his pocket and takes a lotto slip too and he says yes that's fine

Only now I work at an undignified bookstore like a Barnes and Noble with a trans guy similar to Mike in every way or actually he works there I am just a frequent customer and we have a flirtatious vibe he helps me pick out a book there's a road in the bookstore and cars rushing past us but only sometimes, then there's a lull when I pull him or he pulls me into an undignified kiss in dire view of the registers and then he fucks me, I come and can't even remember how, maybe fingering, I go down on him but he complains of physical pain and says don't worry it's an NYU thing

I'm a playwright and writing a book, I am also married, and would dearly like to put the photograph of someone I'm kissing on the cover but I have to wait until the oracle gives me permission, there's a war going on she denies it many times until she says yes all right it's your art too

Before that I enter a massage parlor in Chicago where they break your back and gush that it's supposed to be good for you, I have heard all good things about this place where Keanu Reeves works and I expect I will get my back broken by Keanu and go to lay out my fat wallet on the table

But instead discover that the massage parlor is a prison where I'm teaching but I trigger a code by holding the door open too long and then see schoolchildren lined up for something they had to do inside the prison, Alex and I ask a CO if we're free to leave and he says out of the corner of his mouth *nobody's stopping you* so we walk back down the hill to the tune of a conversation about fighting deforestation, a word in my dream I couldn't even recall

Before that I dream of falling asleep in Cam's arms halfway through a conversation and snapping to and waking up moments too late to say something out of my black-bean eyes, first on the couch then in his bed, he had philosophical disquisitions and all I could do was sleep at the wrong time and wake up shaking the sleep from my eyes like I'm awake I'm awake I'm not being rude I just have the wrong stuff in my eyes and then I did it again

Then I am wandering supermarket aisles on Flatbush Avenue the one near my old apartment and the bus to Riis, I am looking for vegan chocolate and when I find it it comes in a bag like the Domino boxes of brown sugar and labeled SIGETICS but I am willing to forgive their illegal behaviour

kissing R. up a steep hill in the dark where we also sleep in the same bed although he tells me we're not supposed to maybe not even allowed to and then it's our shared birthday we are birthday twins going room to room, the rooms are marked kissing and not kissing

Sitting in Halsey St. apartment in my own room except the room was larger and shaped like a diamond and also underwater and someone else was sitting on my bed like a king, the stove and oven were in my room but neither of them worked they only spouted blue flame constantly and they were also disconnected, the stove on the wall, the oven sailing into the street. Kyle says the drive doesn't work you'll have to use the microwave and holds up a bowl of spinach limp in water and I say no I'm not hungry, thanks, I gave it up

S— M— is fucking one of the boys from *Trainspotting*, not Renton and not Spud, the blond one, they're both strung out and I guess they're fucking in my bathroom cause I can hear them every move and wobble I hang in the foyer texting Cam his boss is here fucking in my apartment, instead of a knob the door has only jagged metal which gashes the wall whenever I open it and also looks like hard pointed shit, will it come off in my hand? No, I guess it won't

I find myself at a table at a party with celebutantes snacking on bags of candy, mine are chocolate-covered something, I consider them idly next to stacks of salami. Is the man next to me Alec Baldwin? His features droop, everyone else looks very excited because someone we know has written something we are toasting but I am only tepidly excited mostly I have designs on seducing the Alec Baldwin writer but oh I feel bad about that then my ankle says nonsense

With Becca on the set of *Bachelor in Paradise*, a woman has lost her husband to drugs or some other accident and gestures happily to her second honeymooning husband swimming athletically out to sea when the camera pans out from the lifeguard chair where we're sitting the waters turn red like punch and a sea creature snaps him up whole, oh, she's off to grieve again but I didn't like it either

Before that I am lining up to take a ferry to see Liz Phair play on an island in Canada, my parents are there, so is my sister, I am possibly a tomboy and somebody says something so cruel to me in my multiple jackets I feel like I have to run away to take a drastic and irrefutable action but I don't, I get in line for the ferry and go below deck bound for Liz and the unspeakable Toronto island

Then Jameson is upset about a pretty person
and insists I find out his name but I actually I
just wanna know his salary

But now I am back at Inferno except one small cubicle is bathed in light and bright gold dust, just underneath the throw of that skylight, like on the set for a music video. Jo is cheering for me driving backwards into the daylight, how I need to do the extra party girl thing of making sure to sleep, have I met their friend the race car driver who does the same? He pulls up, handsome, mustachioed, in the dream he's someone I fucked last night and in the light of day I realize he's Jo's crush with the schnoz and the mustache who their cousin once fucked or loved or both

I fashion a cock out of Rice Krispies and insert it into
my ass and think, hmm, how weird, I was hungry,
then in the dream I say to someone *what a shame
when it looks like a cock but isn't* watching myself get
fucked with Rice Krispies from above

Talking with Stephen who has just appeared in a 20-act Mabou
Mines show with Italian names for each of its complex movements
of desire and kitsch and pain, most of which took place in a deep
pink room with fuzz-covered walls. It's supposed to be Stephen's
big shot to make it Off-Broadway but he seems bored and lonely, a
man is offstage treating him pretty bad, he looks like the guy from
Skins who threatens to cut Sid's balls off. We are on the Williamsburg
Bridge talking and talking, 200 feet in the air, and we are also in
the play's pink room. I say I can't wait to see the previews and he
mostly shrugs, now I've gotta bike home but it takes so long

A breakup happens slowly and imperceptibly between
me, Justin Vivian Bond, and another cabaret singer.
Every time I think we have identified the source of
our discomfort the terms of the conversation shift, or
I realize I broke up with that person years ago but here
is another relationship fresh for loss and Ray tells us
all how television was made from the talking of you
fucking dorks

I am in a school building with Mike, I knew there was gonna be an attack on the school via helicopter but still I run to the bathroom and then I see it pull up and start to fire, it kills the security guard from *Dog Day Afternoon*. I crawl on hands and knees in a circle around the school, constructed like a large open square and then in the front vestibule another creature with machine guns strapped to its back opens fire, Mike who has been sitting alone runs out in mild concern, I say I'm all right, it's the same helicopter you used to court me with when you were Ted Berrigan

I live in an apartment that was my apartment but had an extra room for a blonde girl and Theda Hammel. The super's named Kenny Berkeley, he comes up the stairs to say *hello son* and I point at myself and say *I'm not son*

Before that I am very close to a surgery so I travel to a horrible bourgeois town with Jo, we have no money so we steal an expensive ring and some cash, then I take our host for brunch so they won't notice. A provocateur without a name comes up from downstairs and throws a spoon at us, like a ghost with one function, then before we've packed or even locked the doors to our chambers up the stairs they come en masse throwing glasses and water and mostly damaging their own head. I feel bad about the heist but now the host falls on the table crying and bleeding so really what can I do

Visiting a university I haven't seen before it's up a hill it's a lot of brick and fluorescent lights it looks like a high school with orange carpets it also looks like Rutgers, Holly Raymond is tending the Jack Spicer reading room, you came, she says, with the palpable excitement of a large plant in the sun, here comes one now

Talking with Alex who morphed into Aurora about what Kylie Minogue albums Kevin liked and then I tried to name Kylie's albums and forgot them all even *Aphrodite* even *Fever* even *Confide in Me*

I'm working at a terrible restaurant & sculpture garden with Lix and Andrea and Becca and Neon, it's like a fan fiction version of our lives only with villainy and food particles on the forks instead of puppy love. The owners are stealing our wages and won't give our money back nor the time off work I need for vaginoplasty, in the dream I need it again like a test I passed in waking life and still have to retake over and over

H. like a vampire or a guest his hands all over me in a large house in London, walking up bicycle ramps over large swaths of the city. H. is a guest at a dinner party where the other guests include a mother and daughter, the mother's wearing an awful wig, I'm half-naked and have no breasts but wear David Bowie's wig from *Labyrinth*, H. takes a shine to the daughter and I act as procurer and get the mother off his back, she's a TERF so it isn't easy, all the lights are out we cycle upstairs and down, will he ever kiss me again? Then H. becomes Cam and I am full of praise for his new book

A cooler version of myself both an ecoterrorist and a fellowship headliner runs a dance party on a Sunday night with Andrea then I am back in a childhood home my mom is getting dressed and congratulating me on finishing my degree it's very nice she says and leaves it's her birthday and all her students have arrived my face is so ugly how can I be here

Grindr date descends a long staircase through a park to his apartment it's day but his apartment is dark he's gorgeous taller than me imposing in a filthy apartment we make out and I feel weird he sticks a needle in my arm and I say what the hell did you just put in me and he says relax and then that when we kissed his lips were covered in cocaine that somehow I didn't notice I say fuck you I didn't ask for this I'm graduating today

But when I see Stephen tell him the story and he says oh when I fucked that guy he tried to freak me out by shooting me up with a saline solution as if that made it better I discover a chapbook I printed myself of embarrassing poems at the start of my graduate career in which the titles are academic essays and the words are replaced with dots and dashes

Wanted to sleep with C., in the dream named BC or DC but he was on a date so I ended up sleeping with N., who was mad to be some kind of second choice, we played an elaborate guessing game, a mom came in and told us C. was staying over at his girlfriend's, also she was a realtor in a house where she displayed properties for sale in Hudson, people kept poking their heads in but twice I ended up naked and received a stern warning that I wouldn't be invited back for the wedding

I win a research fellowship only forget to ask for housing show up to an attic the first night surrounded by college students assuming I would have a room so there's nothing it's like *Anastasia* before they leave Russia only anti-communist well so exactly like the movie I am with an old woman but she's sharing the room with another old woman not even the elderly get their own pots to piss in the second introduces herself as Weema, it's like *Grey Gardens* but they're both old, one exits the bathroom she's blown up like a bouncy castle I guess I'll sleep out in the hall

Walking around LA with Zach and an older man is carrying dildos and measuring them we see one that's maybe a yardstick and we want to measure it but our older mentor thinks that would be rude without a baby so both of us say I'm baby

an attitude I did not have days prior when I made out with T. in a dream but he was also H. and wouldn't kiss me back, fully, only press his lips on mine, no tongue a chaste kiss as if embarrassed or in fear or on stage

Before that I dream that an unlikely woman participates in a surfing contest and road trip as an extensive trick to doxx a fascist, on waking I guess it's the plot of *Miss Congeniality* if Sandra Bullock wasn't a cop

Then I'm filling up sandwiches and spreading them on plates, wraps with bean fillings and spinach but I don't eat any of them, a hot ASMR YouTube star asks if I have room. Please, I say, and motion to the plates

At a rest stop many miles in the air I'm smoking with Stephen, wake up briefly with a film score playing in my ears like a staccato opera, I decide I like this dream. Stephen keeps asking if I wanna take a hit put on clothes & come to dinner but I say no I don't wanna eat

I apply for a research fellowship only it turns out to have been cursed from the year before and nobody wanted it and also the entire fellowship it seemed would happen on the Rockaway peninsula and although it was prestigious all you had to do was not complain

Graeme had organized a revolutionary recycling program in which the reuse of old couches and futons contributed directly to revolutionary struggle his cat on a tear around the apartment, in life not the dream, in the dream his cat was the agent of reuse and upcycling, I couldn't interfere with the cat's leaps and scurrying without treachery to the party line

A murder takes place in a large city without a sky, contained in an enormous room. Its disposable arena lies to the side of the city in a second, parallel, room the disposable arena is full of junk, piles of it, sold for scrap the murder takes place out here too, where there are Greek restaurants and a river underneath, of brackish garbage water, is this a place you call Chicago? I know who the murderer is, but have no evidence, I attempt to catch him before he dismembers me. A detective discovers the bodies in the river, and announces to his team that the river has everything to teach them that they can possibly learn about their own city

I am having sex with a white guy who looks like a pastor — dadly, handsome, but somehow asexual, on waking I realize he's the actor who plays Pastor Mike in Mormon Boys, we're not in the Mormon studio we're in a lifeboat in the dream I have a dick again and am pounding on it in my sleep while I dream about this man fucking me unimpressively, and yet I come, loudly, loud enough to wake Rosario up, she must be sleeping in the room next door, and in fact when I wake up I am only edging despite how this man looked like aging noodles

I am listening to an wannabe impressive start-up boss explain how he sent out "millions" of electric fans but he hadn't stolen them, I kept trying to make him a Robin Hood of cheap fans but he disputed the title

Underwater and can't find the surface, at least my calves have pink ombré lights in them, soon I find myself in a rural farm house full of children, catching fire from below. Several naked firefighters rush in, it's like a whole calender has come to life in the heat of crisis

Before that I am bound uptown on a train with Stephen and a woman friend of his, he asks if it's worthwhile to read Brecht and it's weird cause I thought he was part of a big Brecht festival I had just seen but in fact it was a circus, we head there next. I end up having to sleep next to a squid on land, who secretes some sticky black-brown liquid like molasses, it gets on my feet and maybe I have to eat it. A picture of Stephen and his friends, who are pets like Christopher Robin, attempting to carnivorize the squid and its ragtag troupe of a small elephant and some other animals. The faces of the pet-like ragged troupe are fixed in a mask of happy striving, the fish look inscrutable. Then Stephen and his woman friend are in a play I'm late to see, why didn't I plan better

A bimbo-looking plastic hot clone of Lix is gaymous we go to a show and the clone and Lix meet but the clone steals their necklace we drag them out of the movie theatre we never exit instead deposit them at a lecture about the kidnapping which has become famous in a book by Simone White, also it happened in 1820 and I wake up crying for Kevin Killian

Road trip or escape where I encounter A. but no A. you know both of us in rowboats paddling past highway signs independently without shelter, at night you have to stay awake to beat off the wolves who are actually very white fish and the landscape is covered in snow. I ask something like if they can do it on their own without parents, they are already beating wolf-fish away with their shoes, I say well maybe I'll try that

An architect refused to design any longer, in order to prevent gentrification disaster. I saw his designs he was refusing to make, in plexiglass display cases as if in a museum, skyscrapers but very small ones you could fit them in your bag, surrounded by littler buildings, three or four of them bound for Milwaukee

then somebody enumerated for me the essential steps of leaving an apartment; there were four but the only one I remember is leave a forwarding address for your money

Cam moves around plates to defeat Zach in a game of friendship, "friendship" is a dream like chess or life-sized checkers played with pieces representing the components of a life. Here are the playing pieces: black rectangular plates, with deep circular divets, like felted cardboard hats or lightly furred styrofoam containers

Then Eugene Levy was Dodie Bellamy and both were a sometime hippie socialist of books turned successful entrepreneur, Eugene in the form of Dodie in the form of a businessman relates small-business advice in voiceover and I'm lying there a passive audience oh I'm very top-heavy I might faint

On strike at a large school where I am both teacher and a student in high school, divided precisely in half between management and faculty by a line of water bottles, I lecture other students about chanting and regret it immediately

An orgy of men plays out as if on screen but immediately after woven into a tapestry in which cum was threaded into golden braids before it even landed

Katie arrives to sit by my sickbed and comfort
my shredded knee *all I came to let you know is*
that it's pouring and I woke up and it was

I live in another apartment with organizers
from the grad union but we're being harassed
by anti-union leafletters outside the front door,
then I am walking with Candy Darling we
covet lipstick tubes and I'm the named adjunct
on the knife table

With A. skinny in leggings but no A. you know we murder a twink a second clone to Lady Gaga lives out of his blood only she doesn't know who Lady Gaga is one year later I am turning 27 on Lady Gaga's birthday so is A. so's the clone she arrives at a restaurant with her friend a clone of Kim Kardashian they've never watched television been kept off the internet don't know who they look like the Jersey twins of, curvier flat-ironed hair and tanning beds, at the restaurant greeted by friends they don't recognize, attract the attention of the crowd the real LG is on her way to meet her sister-daughter who's looking confused, so confused but gracious under her highlights

Leah hands out inflated plastic shapes as awards for the particular qualities of sleep and wakefulness, sitting at the edge of Mike's bed: yellow stars for charm, silver triangles for impressive dance moves. That's sweet, I think, slipping off the edge of Mike's white noise machine, but why is she watching us sleep?

Notes

MDC refers to Metropolitan Detention Center, a federal prison in Sunset Park, Brooklyn.

Stoffwechsel /ѕнтоғғ•veksel/ is Marx's term for the metabolic exchange between human society and the natural world.

"A Less Exciting Personism," co-authored with Cam Scott, links two simultaneous poems on the occasion of the solar eclipse on August 21, 2017.

"Blind Item" denounces the poet Stephen Ira, who promised to pay me $0.78 for the privilege. Much of the collaged text derives from E.M. Forster's *Howards End*. The claim that machinery *aufhob* or "abolished" handicraft derives from *Capital*, vol. 1.

"Goodnight, Rimbaud" is a distant ekphrasis of the David Wojnarowicz *Rimbaud in NY* series. "Parkade" is a word in Canadian English, meaning a "multistory parking garage."

"Kissing Other People or the House of Fame" is a serial poem written out of a dream journal sustained between April 2019 and April 2020. It derives half of its title from Chaucer's *The House of Fame*, a poem recording the poet's fantastical dreams on "the tenthe day of December." Nobody, Chaucer says, has had "swich a dreem as this." With a couple of permissive exceptions, the poem moves chronologically backwards through the dreams. All of the proper names in the dreams refer to people, except for "Ezra," who is a cat.

Acknowledgements

Prior publication: "Five Dollar Drive" in *HOMINTERN*; "Blind Item" in *Tagvverk*; "Goodnight, Rimbaud" in the *Brooklyn Rail*; an excerpt from "Kissing Other People" in the zine *Panda's Friend*. Many thanks to the editors: Jesi Gaston, Barrett White, Anselm Berrigan, Brandon Brown. Thanks to Astrid Lorange and Andrew Brooks at Rosa Press for publishing the original, Australian, edition of this book, and to Chris Gaul for designing. Thanks to everyone at Nightboat for taking on the US edition of the book.

One of the theses that sustains this book, particularly the title poem, is the sense that dreaming is a social, not a private, act. I'm grateful to everyone who participated in and made vibrant the contexts that in some sense the dreams are a continuation of: yes, you.

Thanks and love to Aaina Amin, Addison Vawters, Becca Teich, Chris Berntsen, Chris Wallace, Hannah Black, Jo Barchi, Katie Liederman, Liam O'Brien, Max Fox, Mike Funk, Rosario Inés, Ry Dunn, Patrick DeDauw, Shiv Kotecha, Stephen Ira, Stiben Vargas, Tracy Rosenthal. Thanks to the non-estate of Geoffrey Chaucer.

Particular thanks to Cam Scott, who read the manuscript at every stage. Danez Smith's workshop at the 2019 Lambda Literary emerging writers retreat led me to collect my recorded dreams together as if they might have something to say to each other; thanks to Danez and the participants in the workshop. Then Suzanne Goldenberg invited me to her Crush reading series in November 2019, when I realized that the cumulative journal was already a poem. Rainer Diana Hamilton has been an energetic correspondent, conversationalist, and co-theorist. Stephen Ira really did offer to pay me $0.78 to denounce him in a poem: I love you, Steve, never change.

NIGHTBOAT BOOKS

Nightboat Books, a nonprofit organization, seeks to develop audiences for writers whose work resists convention and transcends boundaries. We publish books rich with poignancy, intelligence, and risk. Please visit nightboat.org to learn about our titles and how you can support our future publications.

The following individuals have supported the publication of this book. We thank them for their generosity and commitment to the mission of Nightboat Books:

Kazim Ali
Anonymous (4)
Aviva Avnisan
Jean C. Ballantyne
The Robert C. Brooks Revocable Trust
Amanda Greenberger
Rachel Lithgow
Anne Marie Macari
Elizabeth Madans
Elizabeth Motika
Thomas Shardlow
Benjamin Taylor
Jerrie Whitfield & Richard Motika

This book is made possible, in part, by grants from the New York City Department of Cultural Affairs in partnership with the City Council and the New York State Council on the Arts Literature Program.